Playful Poems

That Build Reading Skills

20 Fun-Filled Poems With Reproducibles That Improve Reading
Comprehension, Expand Vocabulary, Teach Spelling & More!

by Kirk Mann

SCHOLASTIC
PROFESSIONAL BOOKS

New York • Toronto • London • Auckland • Sydney
Mexico City • New Delhi • Hong Kong

Dedication

To Sally for planting the seed.
To Lucille for helping me stay in the child's world.
To Ming for her patience.

Cover design by Norma Ortiz

Cover and interior artwork by Robert W. Alley,

except pages 5, 9, 10, and 11 by Patrick Girouard

Interior design by Sydney Wright

ISBN: 0-439-11370-9
Copyright © 2000 by Kirk Mann
All rights reserved.
Printed in the U.S.A.

 # Contents

Introduction

Poetry has the wondrous power to make us giggle, imagine, and learn. In fact, most of us were enjoying poetry well before we were able to read it on our own. Your students are sure to love the poems in *Playful Poems That Build Reading Skills*. They'll want to read them again and again, visiting favorite characters who'll seem like old friends.

Teaching with poetry is easy when you use the reproducibles provided in this resource. The Teacher Page and Student Activity Pages will help you target and teach the essential language skills your students need to learn—reading comprehension, spelling, vocabulary, phonics, writing, and more.

When you and your students share the poems and activities in this book, you'll discover animals and people who find themselves in extraordinary circumstances. And you'll discover how teaching with poetry celebrates language, excites the imagination, and enlivens your reading and writing program.

How to Use This Book

TEACHER PAGES

Introduce and follow up each poem with questions designed to promote thoughtful discussion about poetry and language. You'll find several Before Reading Questions and After Reading Questions on each Teacher Page. You'll also find a writing prompt to help students demonstrate reading comprehension and writing skills.

Before Reading Questions

Help your students bridge the gap between what they know and what they don't by discussing the Before Reading Questions with your class. These questions invite children to link what they already know, feel, and imagine with the poem. Before Reading Questions set children up for successful reading and comprehending of each poem.

After Reading Questions

Use the After Reading Questions to stimulate postreading class

discussions that build reading comprehension and oral language skills. Invite your students to discuss the postreading questions in small groups of three or four. Then meet as a class. Share opinions, ideas, and interpretations. Ask your students to provide evidence from the poem to support their answers.

Writing Prompts

Follow up your class discussions with the instant writing prompts in this book, giving your students creative opportunities to reflect on the poem they've just read and thoroughly discussed. Before inviting your students to begin the writing process, encourage them to reread the poem. Rereading is a great way to get your students thinking about a poem's themes, action, and characters. The prompts are terrific as springboards to journal writing, too! For further practice with writing skills, ask your students to write in complete sentences or paragraph form.

STUDENT ACTIVITY PAGES

After your students read each poem, invite them to complete the reproducible activity pages. Each reproducible activity page is perfect for students to work on independently, in small groups, or as homework.

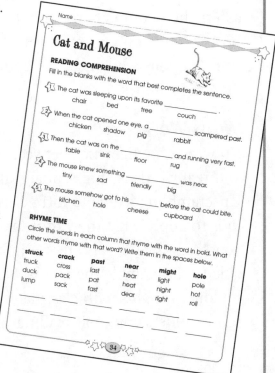

Reading Comprehension

In the Reading Comprehension portion of the student activity pages, students are asked to fill in the blanks with the most appropriate word from the poem. They use their knowledge of the poem to match quotations with characters, key words with lines of poetry, and so on.
Invite your students to use the language of the poem as they problem-solve.

Rhyme Time

Encourage children to practice important rhyming skills with Rhyme Time, where specific words from the poem are grouped with other "special" words. The "special words" are listed on both the poem page and the reproducible student page. In Rhyme Time, your students act as "rhyme detectives" to determine which words rhyme. Then they need to think of two more words that rhyme with the "special word." Take rhyming one step further, and invite your students to use a yellow crayon or highlighter to mark which rhyming words belong in the same word family.

Read, Think, Draw

Here is one creative way to encourage children to think about the poetry they've read, follow simple step-by-step directions, and demonstrate comprehension through visual means. Visual learners are sure to like the Read, Think, Draw Activity. Your students' work will provide you with an opportunity to assess their comprehension of the poem—and you may even get a "sneak peek" at your students' developing drawing abilities.

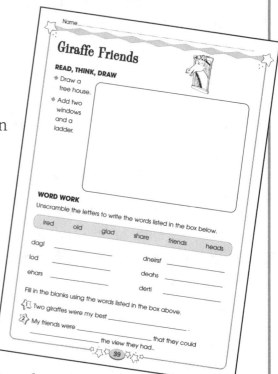

Word Work

Knowing the difference between nonsense words and real words is an essential skill for young readers and writers. Unscrambling letters to form each poem's "special words" is one way for kids to apply what they know about initial letter sounds, word endings, consonant blends, and more. Invite your students to discuss how they were able to unscramble the words. Sharing problem-solving strategies and word-building insights with classmates is a great way for students to build self-confidence in their reading and writing abilities.

Getting the Most From Each Poem

Imagine If

Invite your students to imagine what would happen in a poem if it featured a different animal. Imagine if it was a porcupine helping the farmer in "The Farm Octopus." Imagine if had a been a kangaroo helping to do the housework in "Dino Helps With Housework." Discuss what kinds of unusual things could happen in the poem.

Write Riddles

Have your students practice writing and critical-thinking skills by writing riddles about the poems in *Playful Poems That Build Reading Skills*. For example, ask your students to use two clues from a poem to develop a riddle. (*Who took a sticky seat and had eyes that grew very big?* It was the fly in "Fly Gets Tricked," of course.) Provide each student with a piece of color construction paper. Have kids fold their paper in half and write their riddles on the top flap. Then have them write the riddle's answers and the title of the poem on the inside. If you like, have them illustrate the riddle's answer, too. Post each of the riddles on a bulletin board in your classroom. Your students will enjoy looking for clues and solving one another's riddles.

Illustrate

Show your students an illustration from one of the poems without reading the lines of the poem. Ask them to guess what the poem will be about. *(What clues has the illustrator provided about the subject of the poem? themes? setting?)* Invite your students to act as illustrators, giving you an opportunity to assess comprehension through visual representation. Provide children with paper, crayons, and markers. Then ask all of your students to illustrate the same poem.

You're sure to see a myriad of interpretations. That's okay. Does each student demonstrate a basic knowledge of the characters? setting? action? Encourage your students to revisit the poem as they compose their illustration and to include details from the poem to "show" what they know.

Pantomime

Have groups of children reenact a poem through the age-old art of pantomime. First, divide the class into several groups of three or four. Tell each member of the group what role he or she will play. For instance, in "My Pet Tiger" one student could be Terry T., one a teacher, one the mother, and one the child. When you introduce this activity to younger children, you may want to give guidance as to how to pantomime. For instance, you might suggest the following actions. The tiger could sit quietly and lick its paws. The teacher could use a pointer and write on the chalkboard. The mother could shake her head from side to side, and the child could smile and pat the tiger. Invite your students to guess which poem the pantomime portrays. Discuss other ways various roles could be played.

Create an Adjective Word Wall

Send your students on a hunt for descriptive words within the lines of the poems. First, read the poem aloud with your students. Then list the descriptive words on chart paper as your students name them. Some words they may find in "Ant Take a Cruise" are: *rough, bouncy, steep, nosy,* and *enormous.* Post the list in your writing center as a word wall so that children can readily incorporate them into their writing. If you like, invite your students to use word-wall words in a sentence, a poem, or a short story.

My Funny Octopus

Use the questions and prompt below to encourage your students to discuss and think about the poem.

Before Reading Questions

1. What is special about an octopus? How is an octopus different from a fish?

2. Why do you think octopuses have so many arms?

3. How might life be different for the octopus if he had only four arms?

After Reading Questions

1. How would it feel to have all of Octo's arms around you at once?

2. Which would be more fun, going to a dance with Octo or watching him play the piano?

3. What would it be like to play cards with Octo?

Writing Prompt

✎ Describe what it would be like to have a pet octopus. Where would you keep it? What would you feed it?

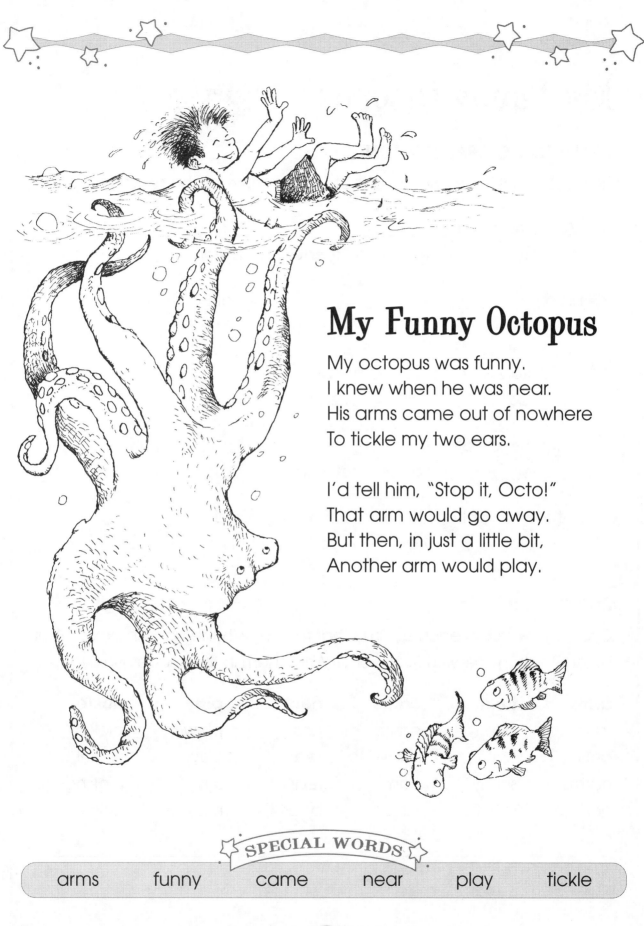

My Funny Octopus

My octopus was funny.
I knew when he was near.
His arms came out of nowhere
To tickle my two ears.

I'd tell him, "Stop it, Octo!"
That arm would go away.
But then, in just a little bit,
Another arm would play.

13

My Funny Octopus

READING COMPREHENSION

Fill in the blanks with the word that best completes the sentence.

1. My octopus was _____ .

      busy   sad   funny   mean

2. His arms _____ out of nowhere.

      ran   came   walked   jumped

3. The octopus's arms tickled my two _____ .

      faces   noses   ears   chins

4. When I said, "Stop it, Octo!," that _____ would go away.

      leg   arm   tooth   octopus

5. But then, in just a little bit, another arm would _____ .

      play   walk   go   skip

RHYME TIME

Circle the words in each column that rhyme with the word in bold. What other words rhyme with that word? Write them in the spaces below.

arms	**funny**	**came**	**near**	**play**	**tickle**
farms	bunny	name	nest	plow	pickle
ants	honey	same	tear	day	nickel
harms	sunny	can	rear	say	picking
cars	money	sand	bear	may	sick

_____ _____ _____ _____ _____ _____

_____ _____ _____ _____ _____ _____

Name ....

My Funny Octopus

READ, THINK, DRAW

◆ Draw an octopus.

◆ Color him purple.

WORD WORK

Unscramble the letters to write the words listed in the box below.

| arms | funny | came | near | play | tickle |

rean _____

sarm _____

ynnfu _____

kletic _____

meac _____

layp _____

Fill in the blanks using the words listed in the box above.

1. The octopus was _____ .

2. The octopus used his _____ to _____ .

The Missing Cookie

Use the questions and prompt below to encourage your students to discuss and think about the poem.

Before Reading Questions

1. Do any of you have a "cookie tooth"?
2. Why do the cookies disappear so fast?
3. Which is best, a glass cookie jar or one that you can't see inside of? Why?

After Reading Questions

1. How could you get Max to share his cookie with you?
2. Did Max eat the cookie? How do you know?
3. Is it possible that the cookie "just walked away" from the jar?

Writing Prompt

✏ Max found a way to get into the cookie jar. How did he do it?

The Missing Cookie

The cookie in the cookie jar
Somehow just walked away.
I wondered who inside our house
Helped cookie get away.

My sister shook her head, "Not me."
My mom said, "Certainly not!"
My dad said, "I can't eat those things.
They make my white teeth rot."

We all looked down at our dog, Max,
Whose eyes told us the truth.
Max somehow had found a way
To feed his cookie tooth.

The Missing Cookie

READING COMPREHENSION

Draw a line to match the sentence
to the person that said it, or to Max.

1 "Not me."   Max

2 "They make my white teeth rot."   Mom

3 "Certainly not!"   Sister

4 His eyes told us the truth.   Dad

RHYME TIME

Circle the words in each column that rhyme with the word in bold. What
other words rhyme with that word? Write them in the spaces below.

jar	shook	head	found	tooth	feed
bar	took	heap	round	toast	seed
far	shop	read	for	truth	need
jaw	cook	bed	sound	toot	fed
car	look	said	pound	booth	bead
___	___	___	___	___	___
___	___	___	___	___	___

The Missing Cookie

READ, THINK, DRAW

◆ Finish drawing the glass cookie jar.

◆ Put some cookies in it.

◆ Draw Max staring at the cookies in the cookie jar.

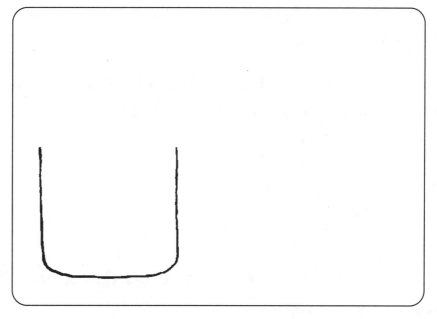

WORD WORK

Unscramble the letters to write the words listed in the box below

| jar | shook | head | found | tooth | feed |

thoot _____   daeh _____

defe _____   raj _____

khoos _____   nfoud _____

Fill in the blanks using the words listed in the box above.

1. The cookie was missing from the cookie _____ .

2. Max _____ a way to _____ his cookie _____ .

Fish's Wish

Use the questions and prompt below to encourage your students to discuss and think about the poem.

Before Reading Questions

1. If you had your wish, what kind of a fish would you like to be?

2. If you were a fish, would you want to live in the ocean, a lake, a pond, or a river? What about a little creek?

3. Have you ever gone fishing? Describe your experience.

After Reading Questions

1. What would you think if you saw a fish flying?

2. How does the fish's father feel?

3. Could fish get his wish? How?

Writing Prompt

✎ If you were a fish, what would you do to keep from getting caught by a fisherman?

Fish's Wish

The fish would gaze into the sky
And wish that he could fly.
The fish would stare off at the beach
And say, "One day I'll try . . ."

"To walk or run or skip or jump
Or play upon the sand."
And then the fish's dad would say,
"You've got to understand . . ."

"You've got a tail and fins and scales.
You live inside the sea.
So stop your dreams of what can't be
And swim around with me."

Fish's Wish

READING COMPREHENSION

Fill in the blanks with the word that best completes the sentence.

1. The fish would gaze into the _____

   water   sun   sky   sea

   and wish that he could _____ .

   eat   fly   rain   talk

2. "One day I'll try to walk or run or skip or jump _____ upon the sand."

   sit   play   bake   jump

3. The fish's dad said, "You've got a tail and fins and _____ ."

   eyes   scales   gills   fur

4. "You live inside the _____ ."

   beach   rocks   sea   clouds

5. "So stop your dreams of what can't be and _____ around with me ."

   dive   swim   float   bite

RHYME TIME

Circle the words in each column that rhyme with the word in bold. What other words rhyme with that word? Write them in the spaces below.

fish	walk	skip	jump	play	sand
dish	talk	ship	lump	day	land
first	rock	hip	jerk	way	stand
wish	clock	sky	bump	stay	sink

_____ _____ _____ _____ _____ _____

_____ _____ _____ _____ _____ _____

Fish's Wish

READ, THINK, DRAW

◆ Draw a fish flying.

◆ Add clouds to your picture.

WORD WORK

Unscramble the letters to write the words listed in the box below.

| fish | walk | skip | jump | play | sand |

hifs _____

dsna _____

ylap _____

pumj _____

aklw _____

piks _____

Fill in the blanks using the words listed in the box above.

☆1 The _____ would gaze into the sky.

☆2 "One day I'll try to _____ or run or _____ or

_____ or play upon the _____ ."

Little Brother and Dogs

Use the questions and prompt below to encourage your students to discuss and think about the poem.

Before Reading Questions

1. What does it feel like to be kissed by a dog?

2. Can a happy dog kiss you and wag her tail at the same time?

3. How does a cat tell you that he likes you?

After Reading Questions

1. Why did the little brother kiss the dog?

2. What do you think the dog thought when the little brother kissed him?

3. Was the dog happy? How do you know?

Writing Prompt

✎ Why do dogs sometimes lick people?

Little Brother and Dogs

When my little brother sees a dog
He seems to lose his mind.
His eyes light up. He points and gurgles,
"Mommy, Mommy, mine!"

The dog runs up with wagging tail
To kiss my brother's face.
My brother seems so happy,
He must like the doggie's taste.

☆ SPECIAL WORDS ☆

sees   dog   mind   wag   tail   face

Little Brother and Dogs

READING COMPREHENSION

Fill in the blanks with the word that best completes the sentence.

1. When my little _____ sees a dog,

   sister   cousin   brother   father

   he seems to lose his _____ .

   hat   mind   socks   food

2. His _____ light up.

   face   hands   eyes   ears

3. The dog runs up to _____ my brother.

   bark   bite   scratch   kiss

4. The dog's tail is _____ .

   itching   sitting   wagging   still

RHYME TIME

Circle the words in each column that rhyme with the word in bold. What other words rhyme with that word? Write them in the spaces below.

sees	dog	mind	wag	tail	face
trees	frog	find	wait	pail	race
sets	dirt	kind	bag	tape	vase
bees	log	mice	rag	sail	faint

_____	_____	_____	_____	_____	_____
_____	_____	_____	_____	_____	_____

Little Brother and Dogs

READR, THINK, DRAW

◆ Draw the dog.

◆ Put a blue collar on his neck.

WORD WORK

Unscramble the letters to write the words listed in the box below.

| sees | dog | mind | wag | tail | face |

efca   _____   eess   _____

dgo   _____   tlia   _____

gaw   _____   dnim   _____

Fill in the blanks using the words listed in the box above.

1. When my little brother _____ a _____ he seems

   to lose his _____ .

2. The dog runs up with wagging _____ to kiss my brother's _____ .

The Farm Octopus

Use the questions and prompt below to encourage your students to discuss and think about the poem.

Before Reading Questions

1. Is the title "The Farm Octopus" strange? Why?

2. How could an octopus become a helper on a farm?

3. Where do octopuses usually live?

After Reading Questions

1. Why did the other farm animals complain about the octopus?

2. Why was it difficult for the octopus to do a good job?

3. How do you think the farmer felt when he took the octopus back to the ocean? Why?

Writing Prompt

✎ Why do you think the octopus might be happier in the ocean?

The Farm Octopus

The farmer's octopus could work
As fast as eight good hands.
The octopus could hoe and feed
And milk and plow the land.

The cow complained, "He milks too fast."
The chicken said, "That's right.
He also gathers up my eggs
Before it's even light!"

The horse said, "When he rides my back
He's always falling off."
The pig oinked, "I once found him
Swimming around inside my trough!"

And so the farmer took the
Octopus back to the sea.
The octopus said, "Don't be sad.
The ocean's home to me."

TO THE
Sea

SPECIAL WORDS

| good | hoe | plow | light | found | took |

The Farm Octopus

READING COMPREHENSION

Fill in the blanks with the word that best completes the sentence.

1. The octopus could work as fast as _____ good hands.

      two   five   six   eight

2. He could hoe and feed and milk and _____ the land.

      rake   seed   plow   water

3. The cow complained, "He _____ too fast."

      walks   swims   milks   eats

4. The chicken said, "He gathers up my eggs before the day is even _____ !"

      over   light   here   ready

5. The _____ said, "When he rides my back, he's always falling off."

      bull   horse   hen   duck

RHYME TIME

Circle the words in each column that rhyme with the word in bold. What other words rhyme with that word? Write them in the spaces below.

good	**hoe**	**plow**	**light**	**found**	**took**
wood	toe	how	night	around	cook
stood	sew	please	like	hound	shook
could	row	bow	right	four	book
_____	_____	_____	_____	_____	_____
_____	_____	_____	_____	_____	_____

Name ....

The Farm Octopus

TO THE Sea ➤➤

READ, THINK, DRAW

◆ Draw the pig's trough.

◆ Show the octopus swimming inside it.

WORD WORK

Unscramble the letters to write the words listed in the box below.

good	hoe	plow	light	found	took

thgil   _____   heo   _____

doog   _____   pwol   _____

koot   _____   dnufo   _____

Fill in the blanks using the words listed in the box above.

1. "He gathers up my eggs before it's even _____ !"

2. The farmer _____ the octopus back to the sea.

Cat and Mouse

Use the questions and prompt below to encourage your students to discuss and think about the poem.

Before Reading Questions

1. Why do you think mice usually come out at night?

2. Why would a mouse rather live in a house with a dog than in one with a cat?

3. If you were a mouse, what kind of a home would you want to live in?

After Reading Questions

1. What do you think the cat would do if the mouse turned around and bit him?

2. Why would the mouse like it if the cat wore a collar with a bell?

3. What can the mouse do to keep from ever getting caught?

Writing Prompt

✎ Would you rather be a cat or a mouse? Why?

Cat and Mouse

Our cat was sleeping quietly
Upon her favorite couch.
The clock had just struck midnight
When she thought she heard a mouse.

She opened one eye just a crack.
A shadow scampered past.
And then our cat was on the floor
And running very fast.

The mouse knew something big was near
And ran with all its might.
It felt the cat's hot breath
And knew that soon sharp claws would strike.

The mouse somehow got to its hole
Before the cat could bite.
And hiding there it thought,
"I almost fed the cat tonight."

SPECIAL WORDS

struck	crack	past	near	might

Cat and Mouse

READING COMPREHENSION

Fill in the blanks with the word that best completes the sentence.

1 The cat was sleeping upon its favorite _____ .

      chair   bed   tree   couch

2 When the cat opened one eye, a _____ scampered past.

      chicken   shadow   pig   rabbit

3 Then the cat was on the _____ and running very fast.

      table   sink   floor   rug

4 The mouse knew something _____ was near.

      tiny   sad   friendly   big

5 The mouse somehow got to its _____ before the cat could bite.

      kitchen   hole   cheese   cupboard

RHYME TIME

Circle the words in each column that rhyme with the word in bold. What other words rhyme with that word? Write them in the spaces below.

struck	**crack**	**past**	**near**	**might**	**hole**
truck	cross	last	hear	light	pole
duck	pack	pat	heat	night	hot
lump	sack	fast	dear	right	roll
_____	_____	_____	_____	_____	_____
_____	_____	_____	_____	_____	_____

Cat and Mouse

READ, THINK, DRAW

◆ Draw a
sleeping cat.

◆ Color the
cat orange.

WORD WORK

Unscramble the letters to write the words listed in the box below.

struck	crack	past	near	might	hole

ptsa   _____

loeh   _____

trucks   _____

tighm   _____

kracc   _____

raen   _____

Fill in the blanks using the words listed in the box above.

1. The clock _____ midnight.

2. The cat opened one eye just a _____ and a shadow scampered past.

Giraffe Friends

Use the questions and prompt below to encourage your students to discuss and think about the poem.

Before Reading Questions

1. Have you ever seen a giraffe? Where?

2. If a giraffe had a sore throat, why would it be worse than a stubbed toe?

3. If I wanted to borrow your ladder and you lent me two giraffes, why would I be surprised?

After Reading Questions

1. Would you rather climb a giraffe's neck or a ladder?

2. What do you think the girl and the giraffes ate when they had their jungle feast?

3. What could the girl do if the giraffes were not nearby and she wanted to leave her tree house?

Writing Prompt

✎ Would you like to have a tree house? Why or why not?

Giraffe Friends

When I lived in the jungle
My best friends were two giraffes.
They helped me build my tree house
From a tired old wooden raft.

I used their necks as ladders.
They both said it made them glad
That they could help me get up high
And share the view they had.

Then when my house was finished
We all had a jungle feast.
Their heads poked in my windows
And we danced like jungle beasts.

SPECIAL WORDS

tired   old   glad   share   friends   heads

Giraffe Friends

READING COMPREHENSION

Fill in the blanks with the word that best completes the sentence.

1. When I lived in the _____ , my best friends were two giraffes.

   desert   jungle   mountains   lake

2. They helped me build my tree house from a tired _____ wooden raft.

   new   old   broken   big

3. I used their _____ as ladders.

   backs   legs   necks   feet

4. The giraffes were glad to help me get up high and _____ the view they had.

   see   watch   share   hide

5. When my house was finished, we had a jungle _____ .

   lunch   feast   breakfast   dinner

RHYME TIME

Circle the words in each column that rhyme with the word in bold. What other words rhyme with that word? Write them in the spaces below.

tired	**old**	**glad**	**share**	**friends**	**heads**
hired	told	mad	care	sends	beds
tore	sold	glide	show	bends	sheds
fired	off	sad	bear	free	heal

_____ _____ _____ _____ _____ _____

_____ _____ _____ _____ _____ _____

Giraffe Friends

READ, THINK, DRAW

◆ Draw a tree house.

◆ Add two windows and a ladder.

WORD WORK

Unscramble the letters to write the words listed in the box below.

tired	old	glad	share	friends	heads

dagl _____

lod _____

ehars _____

dneirsf _____

deahs _____

derti _____

Fill in the blanks using the words listed in the box above.

1. Two giraffes were my best _____ .

2. My friends were _____ that they could _____ the view they had.

My Pet Tiger

Use the questions and prompt below to encourage your students to discuss and think about the poem.

Before Reading Questions

1. What would your mother or father say if you brought home a pet tiger?

2. Where would your pet tiger sleep?

3. What games would you and the tiger play together?

After Reading Questions

1. Where does Terry T. come from?

2. Why does everyone at school like him?

3. Does Terry T. love the child? How do you know?

Writing Prompt

✎ If you took a pet tiger to school, what do you think your teacher would say?

My Pet Tiger

I have a little tiger.
His name is Terry T.
We found him in the neighborhood
But now he stays with me.

We get up in the morning.
We have our bowl of mush.
Then afterward I brush our teeth
And off to school we rush.

He'll sit there in the corner.
The teacher doesn't mind,
For Terry watches as I work
Until it's recess time.

Then everybody likes to play
With Terry on the grass.
He chases them and they chase him
And he can run so fast.

He really is my best friend.
I think he loves me too,
Though Mommy says with Terry here
We're living in a zoo.

SPECIAL WORDS

| mush | teeth | time | chase | fast | love |

My Pet Tiger

READING COMPREHENSION

Fill in the blanks with the word that best completes the sentence.

1 Terry is a _____ .

      fish   pig   tiger   lion

2 We _____ Terry T. in the neighborhood.

      heard   ate   found   watched

3 Every morning, we have our _____ of mush.

      jar   can   bowl   cup

4 Who brushes Terry's teeth? _____

      my mother   Terry   me   my brother

5 Terry T. sits in the _____ while I work at school.

      water   chair   corner   front

RHYME TIME

Circle the words in each column that rhyme with the word in bold. What other words rhyme with that word? Write them in the spaces below.

mush	teeth	time	chase	fast	love
crush	tease	dime	face	mast	shove
ring	wreath	dim	race	last	long
_____	_____	_____	_____	_____	_____
_____	_____	_____	_____	_____	_____

My Pet Tiger

READ, THINK, DRAW

- Put mush in Terry T.'s bowl.

- Draw Terry T.

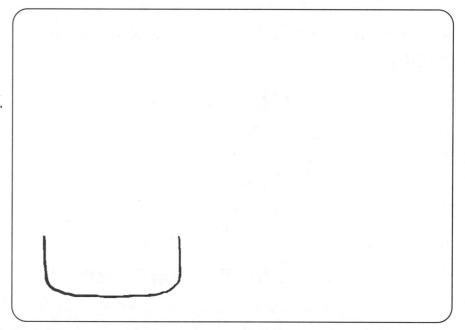

WORD WORK

Unscramble the letters to write the words listed in the box below.

| mush | teeth | time | chase | fast | love |

hteet _____   tsaf _____

eolv _____   hcsae _____

shum _____   emit _____

Fill in the blanks using the words listed in the box above.

1 Each morning, Terry T. and I have our bowl of _____ .

2 Terry T. can run so _____ .

The Hungry Snake

Use the questions and prompt below to encourage your students to discuss and think about the poem.

Before Reading Questions

1. When you see a snake, do you stop to pet it? Why or why not?

2. Why are some people afraid of snakes?

3. Why is it hard for snakes to hop or skip?

After Reading Questions

1. If you had a hopping, leaping, singing snake, what would you do with it?

2. At the end of the poem, the snake is lying down to rest. What would you tell the snake to eat next?

3. Why is the snake scared?

Writing Prompt

✎ If you could be a snake, what kind would you like to be? big or small? poisonous or harmless?

The Hungry Snake

The snake ate a rabbit
And suddenly hopped.
He said, "I am seasick,
This hopping must stop."

He let out the rabbit
Then ate a big frog
And found himself leaping
Right over a log.

Snake said, "I can't take it,
This leaping's no good."
He let out the frog,
Hoping frog understood.

He ate a small bird
From its feet to its beak
Then found himself starting
To sing and to speak.

He let the bird go
And laid down for a rest.
"I'm hungry," he thought,
"But I'm scared of what's next."

SPECIAL WORDS

snake   hopping   leaping   ate   sing   scared

The Hungry Snake

READING COMPREHENSION

Fill in the blanks with the word that best completes the sentence.

1. The snake hopped after eating the _____ .

   frog   bird   rabbit

2. The snake leaped over a log after he ate the big

   _____ .

   frog   bird   rabbit

3. The snake started to sing and speak after he ate the small

   _____ .

   frog   bird   rabbit

RHYME TIME

Circle the words in each column that rhyme with the word in bold. What other words rhyme with that word? Write them in the spaces below.

snake	**hopping**	**leaping**	**ate**	**sing**	**scared**
rake	stopping	heaping	plate	sip	shared
bake	hen	sleeping	late	wing	dared
back	popping	keeping	at	ring	scold
_____	_____	_____	_____	_____	_____
_____	_____	_____	_____	_____	_____

The Hungry Snake

READ, THINK, DRAW

◆ Draw the snake singing.

WORD WORK

Unscramble the letters to write the words listed in the box below.

| snake | hopping | leaping | ate | sing | scared |

eta   _____   pophing _____

gnsi   _____   ekans   _____

pealing _____   deracs   _____

Fill in the blanks using the words listed in the box above.

⭐1 The _____ ate a rabbit and said, "This _____ must stop."

⭐2 The snake _____ a frog and found himself _____. right over a log.

Dino Helps With Housework

Use the questions and prompt below to encourage your students to discuss and think about the poem.

Before Reading Questions

1. If there were a dinosaur in this room now, what would you do?

2. Why don't you find dinosaurs at the zoo?

3. Why do people like to study dinosaurs?

After Reading Questions

1. Why did the mother tell Dino her child could not play?

2. What were three of the child's chores? Name them.

3. Would you want Dino to help you do your housework? Why or why not?

Writing Prompt

✎ If dinosaurs were alive today, where do you think they would live?

Dino Helps With Housework

Mommy, Dino's at our door,
He says he wants to play.
"Tell him you've got chores
To do and cannot play today."

Mommy, Dino wants to help,
He says he knows a lot.
"Ask him if he vacuums rooms
And washes dirty pots."

Mommy, Dino says he'll help,
But doesn't know those things.
Maybe if I show him how
We'll quickly get them clean.

Dino, Mommy says come in,
Now here, you take the broom.
I'll go get the dust pan.
Let's go start inside my room.

Sweep and vacuum, then we dust,
And scrub the pots and pans.
Dino, I'm so proud of you
And all your helping hands.

Mom, can we go out to play?
Dino thinks we're through.
Dino, Mom says it's okay,
Come on, I'll race with you.

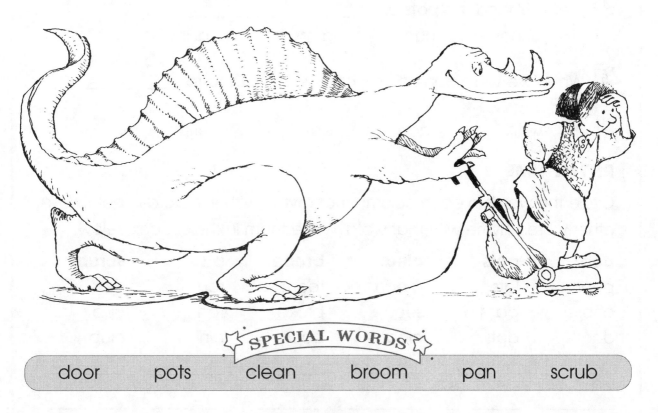

SPECIAL WORDS

door   pots   clean   broom   pan   scrub

Dino Helps With Housework

READING COMPREHENSION

Fill in the blanks with the word that best completes the sentence.

1. "Tell him you've got _____ to do and cannot play today."

   chores   fun   cooking   homework

2. When Dino came in the house, I said, "Now here, you take the
   _____ ."

   broom   mop   toast   candy

3. Dino and I started cleaning inside my _____ .

   kitchen   room   closet   bathroom

4. We scrubbed the pots and _____ .

   dishes   cups   glasses   pans

5. When we were done doing chores, I told Dino to _____
   with me.

   walk   race   eat   drink

RHYME TIME

Circle the words in each column that rhyme with the word in bold. What
other words rhyme with that word? Write them in the spaces below.

door	pots	clean	broom	pan	scrub
poor	lots	mean	room	ran	rub
chore	pans	seen	broke	fan	cub
dog	dots	clear	boom	pin	club
_____	_____	_____	_____	_____	_____
_____	_____	_____	_____	_____	_____

Dino Helps With Housework

READ, THINK, DRAW

◆ Draw Dino helping with housework.

◆ Color Dino red.

WORD WORK

Unscramble the letters to write the words listed in the box below.

door	pots	clean	broom	pan	scrub

neacl _____

bmoor _____

rood _____

stop _____

npa _____

burcs _____

Fill in the blanks using the words listed in the box above.

1. "Ask him if he washes dirty _____ ."

2. You take the _____ , I'll go get the dust _____ .

If Dogs Could Talk

Use the questions and prompt below to encourage your students to discuss and think about the poem.

Before Reading Questions

1. Do dogs understand what people say to them?

2. Why do dogs growl?

3. Why do dogs wag their tails?

After Reading Questions

1. How would things be different if dogs could talk?

2. Can you give a happy bark? a bark to scare? a bark that shows you are lonesome?

3. Why would the dog in the poem "have a lot to say" to the family?

Writing Prompt

✎ What would you do if a dog called you on the telephone? What would you tell him?

If Dogs Could Talk

If dogs could talk I think our dog
Would have a lot to say.
He'd probably tell my little brother,
"SIT and now just STAY."

He'd probably tell my sister,
"How about an ice cream cone?"
He'd probably tell my mother,
"Please go get me a big bone."

He'd probably tell my father,
"Make a left turn up ahead."
He'd probably tell me, "Kid, tonight
I'm sleeping in your bed."

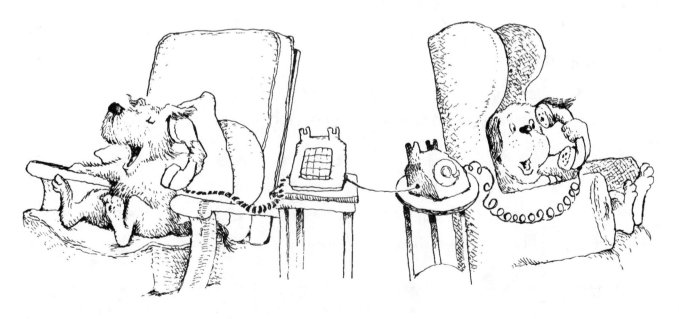

SPECIAL WORDS

dog   sit   stay   bone   kid   bed

If Dogs Could Talk

READING COMPREHENSION

Fill in the blanks with the word that best completes the sentence.

1. He'd probably tell my little brother, " _____ and now just STAY!"

   WALK   RUN   SIT   EAT

2. He'd probably tell my sister, "How about an ice cream _____ ?"

   cake   pie   bar   cone

3. He'd probably tell my _____ , "Please, go get me a big bone."

   father   me   mother   sister

4. He'd probably tell my father, "Make a _____ turn up ahead."

   fast   right   left   slow

RHYME TIME

Circle the words in each column that rhyme with the word in bold. What other words rhyme with that word? Write them in the spaces below.

dog	**sit**	**stay**	**bone**	**kid**	**bed**
log	bit	day	cone	lid	fed
frog	see	say	alone	did	led
do	fit	stop	none	hid	beg
_____	_____	_____	_____	_____	_____
_____	_____	_____	_____	_____	_____

If Dogs Could Talk

READ, THINK, DRAW

◆ Draw the
   dog sleeping.

◆ Give him
   a big bone.

WORD WORK

Unscramble the letters to write the words listed in the box below.

dog	sit	stay	bone	kid	bed

dbe   _____   eonb   _____

ysta   _____   ogd   _____

tis   _____   idk   _____

Fill in the blanks using the words listed in the box above.

1. The _____ would probably tell my little brother to

   "_____ and now just _____ ."

2. The dog would probably tell my mother, "Please go get me a big

   _____ ."

City Mouse

Use the questions and prompt below to encourage your students to discuss and think about the poem.

Before Reading Questions

1. Why is a mouse afraid of a cat?

2. Would you rather play with a cat or a mouse?

3. If you were a mouse, what kind of house or apartment would you want to live in?

After Reading Questions

1. What was the good advice that the mother mouse gave the little mouse?

2. Why is this one a lucky mouse?

3. Where do you think this mouse finds food to eat?

Writing Prompt

✎ Do you think that cats and mice will ever be friends? Why or why not?

City Mouse

When I was just a little mouse
I ran off to the city.
My mom said I wouldn't like it.
I'd be eaten by a kitty.

It's true, some cats came after me
And yet I dodged them all.
And now I have a home inside
A nice apartment wall.

And some nights when it's cold outside
I'm thankful to my toes
That I have crumbs and cheese right here
Beneath my whiskered nose.

SPECIAL WORDS

mouse   city   wall   cheese   cold   toes

City Mouse

READING COMPREHENSION

Fill in the blanks with the word that best completes the sentence.

1. When he was just a _____ mouse, he ran off to the city.
   big   gray   little   fat

2. His mom said he'd be _____ by a kitty.
   seen   grabbed   eaten   bit

3. When cats came after the mouse, he _____ them all.
   chased   ate   dodged   sniffed

4. The mouse had a home in an apartment _____ .
   room   kitchen   floor   wall

5. The mouse had a _____ nose.
   fat   whiskered   tall   funny

RHYME TIME

Circle the words in each column that rhyme with the word in bold. What other words rhyme with that word? Write them in the spaces below.

mouse	city	wall	cheese	cold	toes
house	kitty	tall	trees	cob	tops
more	witty	fall	chair	sold	bows
mice	sip	bat	tease	told	hose
map	kind	ball	peas	bold	rose

____   ____   ____   ____   ____   ____

____   ____   ____   ____   ____   ____

City Mouse

READ, THINK, DRAW

◆ Draw the city mouse's home.

WORD WORK

Unscramble the letters to write the words listed in the box below.

| mouse | city | wall | cheese | cold | toes |

lalw _____

ticy _____

usemo _____

soet _____

seeech _____

dloc _____

Fill in the blanks using the words listed in the box above.

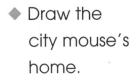 The _____ ran off to the _____ .

When it was _____ outside, the mouse was thankful to

his _____ .

Up the Elephant's Trunk

Use the questions and prompt below to encourage your students to discuss and think about the poem.

Before Reading Questions

1. How is an elephant different from other animals?

2. What are three ways an elephant uses its trunk?

3. How would an elephant's life be different if it had a short nose instead of a long trunk?

After Reading Questions

1. Why would peanut shells be in the elephant's trunk?

2. Why did the mouse help the elephant?

3. How did the elephant feel after his trunk was scratched?

Writing Prompt

✎ Would you have helped the elephant? Why or why not?

Up the Elephant's Trunk

The elephant once said to me,
"Mouse, please climb in my nose
And go until I say to stop,
Then scratch there with your toes."

I climbed inside the long, deep trunk,
The air was damp and gray.
I walked across some peanut shells
And grass and bits of hay.

Then halfway up the bumpy trail
The elephant yelled, "Stop!"
"Scratch!" he said. "With all your might,
Just jump and kick and hop."

I scratched and itched and itched and scratched,
He finally yelled, "Enough!"
And then he blew me out his trunk
With lots of other stuff.

The elephant gave one big laugh
And said, "I thank you much."
And then he put his trunk on me
And gave me a warm touch.

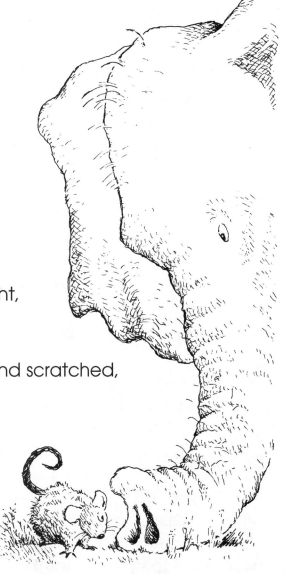

SPECIAL WORDS

nose   long   trunk   damp   bumpy   trail

Up the Elephant's Trunk

READING COMPREHENSION

Fill in the blanks with the word that best completes the sentence.

1. The elephant said, "Mouse, please _____ inside my nose."

    walk   jump   climb   get

2. I walked across some peanut _____ .

    crumbs   shells   leaves   butter

3. Halfway up the bumpy _____ , the elephant yelled, "Stop!"

    road   path   street   trail

4. "Scratch!," he said. "With all your might, just jump and kick and _____ ."

    hop   stomp   step   fall

5. He finally _____ , "Enough!"

    said   cried   yelled   shouted

RHYME TIME

Circle the words in each column that rhyme with the word in bold. What other words rhyme with that word? Write them in the spaces below.

nose	**long**	**trunk**	**damp**	**bumpy**	**trail**
not	song	dunk	camp	lumpy	pail
goes	lone	sunk	ramp	humpy	sail
bows	wrong	truck	dump	puppy	trail

_____ _____ _____ _____ _____ _____

_____ _____ _____ _____ _____ _____

Up the Elephant's Trunk

READ, THINK, DRAW

◆ Draw the mouse inside the elephant's trunk.

WORD WORK

Unscramble the letters to write the words listed in the box below.

| nose | long | trunk | damp | bumpy | trail |

pmda _____   knurt _____

glno _____   ypmub _____

liart _____   enso _____

Fill in the blanks using the words listed in the box above.

1. The air in the trunk was _____ and gray.

2. Halfway up the _____ , the elephant yelled, "Stop!"

Fly Gets Tricked

Use the questions and prompt below to encourage your students to discuss and think about the poem.

Before Reading Questions

1. Where do you find spider webs?

2. How does keeping a clean web help a spider catch a fly?

3. How can a spider tell when a fly is caught in its web?

After Reading Questions

1. What do you think was in the summer soup that the fly was invited to eat?

2. If you were a fly, and you had been invited to dinner and learned they were serving "fly crunch" for dessert, how would you feel?

3. How do you think the fly felt when the spider yelled, "Hurray"?

Writing Prompt

✎ Would you rather be a smart fly or a smart spider? Why?

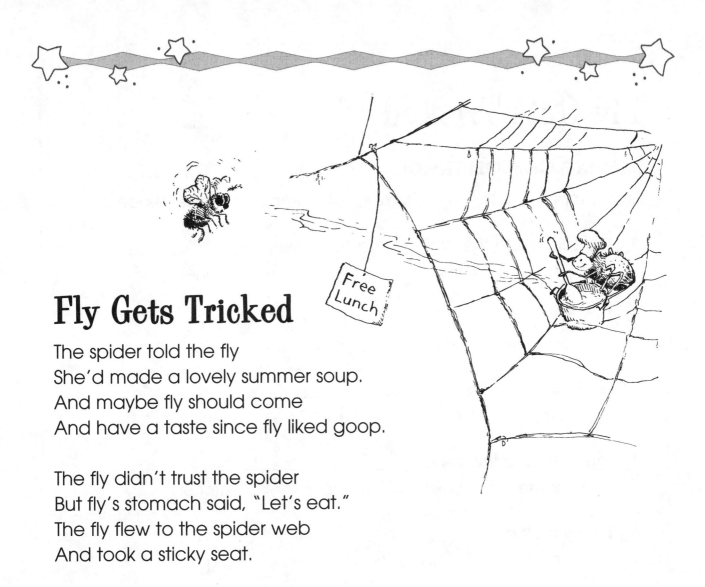

Fly Gets Tricked

The spider told the fly
She'd made a lovely summer soup.
And maybe fly should come
And have a taste since fly liked goop.

The fly didn't trust the spider
But fly's stomach said, "Let's eat."
The fly flew to the spider web
And took a sticky seat.

The spider said, "I'm glad you've come
To share this lovely lunch.
And by the way, did I tell you
Dessert will be fly crunch?"

The fly's small eyes grew very big.
He tried to fly away.
Alas, he found that he was stuck,
And spider yelled, "Hurray!"

SPECIAL WORDS

| fly | made | trust | seat | glad | crunch |

Fly Gets Tricked

READING COMPREHENSION

Fill in the blanks with the word that best completes the sentence.

1. The spider told the fly she'd made a lovely _____ .

   stew   soup   snack   dinner

2. The fly didn't _____ the spider.

   like   hear   trust   see

3. But fly's stomach said, "Let's _____ ."

   drink   chew   eat   think

4. The fly flew to the spider _____ .

   house   web   table   kitchen

5. The fly took a _____ seat.

   small   sticky   tiny   big

RHYME TIME

Circle the words in each column that rhyme with the word in bold. What other words rhyme with that word? Write them in the spaces below.

fly	**made**	**trust**	**seat**	**glad**	**crunch**
shy	shade	dust	meat	sad	bunch
flew	map	true	seed	had	hunch
why	stayed	must	beat	glow	cry

_____ _____ _____ _____ _____ _____

_____ _____ _____ _____ _____ _____

Fly Gets Tricked

READ, THINK, DRAW

◆ Draw a spiderweb.

◆ Draw the fly on his sticky seat.

◆ Draw the spider watching the fly.

WORD WORK

Unscramble the letters to write the words listed in the box below.

| fly | made | trust | seat | glad | crunch |

dagl _____

ylf _____

stae _____

tsurt _____

hcncur _____

edam _____

Fill in the blanks using the words listed in the box above.

1 The spider _____ a lovely summer soup.

2 The fly didn't _____ the spider, but fly's stomach said, "Let's eat."

Sunday on the Farm

Use the questions and prompt below to encourage your students to discuss and think about the poem.

Before Reading Questions

1. Why is it a good idea to eat breakfast every morning?

2. Why don't all the animals on the farm eat the same breakfast?

3. Is Sunday a special breakfast day at your home? Why or why not?

After Reading Questions

1. Why is Sunday a special day on the farm?

2. With which animal in the poem would you like to share breakfast?

3. Do you think the animals liked their Sunday breakfasts? Why or why not?

Writing Prompt

✎ What do you think the farmer has for his breakfast on Sundays?

Sunday on the Farm

Sundays farmer made his friends
The breakfasts of their choice
Making sure that lots of juice
Was there to keep things moist.

"Pig, what will it be today?"
Pig said, "French toast, please."
"Cow, what will you have today?"
"Pancakes mixed with leaves."

"Goat and horse, your mush, of course,
With warm toast on the side.
Duck, you'll get your snails and worms
Chopped up with grass and fried."

"Hen and rooster, fruit with grain,
Eggs for sheep and lamb."
And then the farmer served them all
And said, "How pleased I am."

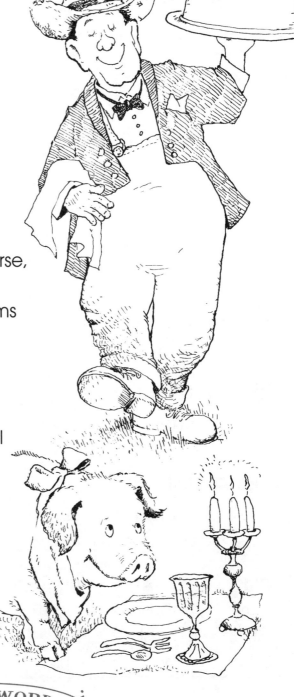

☆ SPECIAL WORDS ☆

| pig | toast | mush | goat | snails | sheep |

Sunday on the Farm

READING COMPREHENSION

Fill in the blanks with the word that best completes the sentence.

1. On _____ , farmer made his friends the breakfasts of their choice.

   Mondays   Sundays   Tuesdays   birthdays

2. The pig wanted _____ .

   eggs   ham   potatoes   French toast

3. Goat and _____ got mush.

   pig   sheep   lamb   horse

4. Hen and rooster got _____ with grain.

   fried   baked   fruit   fresh

5. Sheep and lamb got _____ .

   eggs   soup   meat   vegetables

RHYME TIME

Circle the words in each column that rhyme with the word in bold. What other words rhyme with that word? Write them in the spaces below.

pig	toast	mush	goat	snails	sheep
dig	roast	crush	boat	pails	sleep
pit	most	rush	coat	tails	shine
big	boast	gush	good	nails	keep

___	___	___	___	___	___
___	___	___	___	___	___

Sunday on the Farm

READ, THINK, DRAW

◆ Draw the pig's plate.

◆ Color your picture.

WORD WORK

Unscramble the letters to write the words listed in the box below.

| pig | toast | mush | goat | snails | sheep |

gip _____

gtao _____

hsmu _____

pseeh _____

tsaot _____

slians _____

Fill in the blanks using the words listed in the box above.

1. The _____ and horse ate _____ .

2. The duck ate _____ and worms.

Ant Takes a Cruise

Use the questions and prompt below to encourage your students to discuss and think about the poem.

Before Reading Questions

1. Do you know what *ants* are?

2. What do you do when you find ants in your house?

3. Why is it easy to find where ants are going?

After Reading Questions

1. Why do you think the ant crawled into the bottle?

2. What do you think the ant ate during his trip?

3. Did anyone on the ship hear when the ant yelled, "Set me free"? Why or why not?

Writing Prompt

✎ How would you describe what an ant looks like to someone who has never seen one before?

Ant Takes a Cruise

The ant crawled in a bottle
That fell into the lake.
The ant soon came to realize
She'd made a big mistake.

The lake got rough and bouncy.
The bottle hit a rock.
It went down a steep waterfall
That left the ant in shock.

She stared out of her window
At two big nosy fish.
They saw by ant's enormous eyes
That ant was new to this.

The ant rode down the river
And finally out to sea.
And when at last a ship came near
The ant yelled, "Set me free!"

☆ SPECIAL WORDS ☆

ant	lake	hit	rock	made	stared

Ant Takes a Cruise

READING COMPREHENSION

Fill in the blanks with the word that best completes the sentence.

1. The ant crawled in a _____ .

   can   box   bottle   jar

2. The bottle first fell into a _____ .

   puddle   hole   lake   creek

3. In the lake, the bottle hit a _____ .

   log   boat   ship   rock

4. The bottle went down a _____ waterfall.

   calm   little   quiet   steep

5. The ant stared out of his window at two nosy _____ .

   turtles   frogs   fish   snakes

RHYME TIME

Circle the words in each column that rhyme with the word in bold. What other words rhyme with that word? Write them in the spaces below.

ant	**lake**	**hit**	**rock**	**made**	**stared**
can't	make	fit	ring	wade	cared
pant	shake	him	lock	shade	star
dance	lamb	sit	sock	mad	dared
_____	_____	_____	_____	_____	_____
_____	_____	_____	_____	_____	_____

Ant Takes a Cruise

READt, THINK, DRAW

- ◆ Draw the bottle going over the waterfall.

- ◆ Put the ant inside.

WORD WORK

Unscramble the letters to write the words listed in the box below.

> ant   lake   hit   rock   made   stared

ith   _____   edam   _____

eakl   _____   tan   _____

derats   _____   kocr   _____

Fill in the blanks using the words listed in the box above.

1. The _____ crawled in a bottle that fell into the _____ .

2. The lake got rough and the bottle _____ a _____ .

Horse Helps Farmer

Use the questions and prompt below to encourage your students to discuss and think about the poem.

Before Reading Questions

1. Why do people and animals sometimes get sick?

2. How do you feel when you're sick?

3. How do farm animals stay healthy?

After Reading Questions

1. How did the horse know that the farmer was sick?

2. What might have happened if the horse hadn't helped the farmer?

3. How did the horse show that he was thoughtful and kind?

Writing Prompt

✎ How could you tell that the farmer was kind to the animals on his farm?

Horse Helps Farmer

One day the farmer didn't feel well.
He stayed inside his bed.
The horse thought, "Something's wrong
Or he'd be here with us instead."

The horse had hen unlatch the gate.
Then horse ran to the house.
He climbed up farmer's steps
But NOT as quiet as a mouse.

The horse went in the kitchen
And made farmer a warm broth.
He carried it toward farmer's room
Where he heard farmer's cough.

The farmer had a fever,
He was glad to see his friend.
The farmer drank the warm, dark broth
And soon began to mend.

He told the horse, "You've helped me,
Now go back out to your stall.
And please tell everyone
I'll soon be out to feed them all."

SPECIAL WORDS

well   bed   gate   drank   dark   mend

Horse Helps Farmer

READING COMPREHENSION

Fill in the blanks with the word that best completes the sentence.

1. One day the farmer didn't feel _____ .

   sad   thirsty   well   hungry

2. The _____ stayed in bed.

   horse   cow   farmer   pig

3. The horse had _____ unlatch the gate.

   duck   sheep   goose   hen

4. The horse went in the kitchen and made a warm _____ .

   soup   broth   cake   sandwich

5. He carried it toward farmer's room where he heard farmer's

   _____ .

   laugh   cry   television   cough

RHYME TIME

Circle the words in each column that rhyme with the word in bold. What other words rhyme with that word? Write them in the spaces below.

well	**bed**	**gate**	**drank**	**dark**	**mend**
tell	red	late	sank	park	man
fell	ball	date	thank	shark	send
week	said	wait	spank	dare	lend

____ ____ ____ ____ ____ ____

____ ____ ____ ____ ____ ____

Horse Helps Farmer

READ, THINK, DRAW

◆ Draw a bowl of broth.

◆ Color the broth yellow.

WORD WORK

Unscramble the letters to write the words listed in the box below.

well	bed	gate	drank	dark	mend

drak _____   geta _____

llew _____   dnem _____

dbe _____   knard _____

Fill in the blanks using the words listed in the box above.

1 One day, the farmer didn't feel _____ so he stayed

   inside his _____ .

2 The farmer _____ the warm, dark broth.

Our Rhino

Use the questions and prompt below to encourage your students to discuss and think about the poem.

Before Reading Questions

1. Have you ever seen a rhino? Where?

2. If you had a rhino, where would you keep it?

3. Would your family like to have a pet rhino? Why or why not?

After Reading Questions

1. What kinds of food did the rhino in the poem like to eat?

2. What are some ways the dog and the rhino could play together?

3. How did the neighbors feel about the rhino? Why?

Writing Prompt

✎ What would make the rhino REALLY angry?

Our Rhino

Our rhino lived in our backyard.
He liked to eat a lot.
He ate the trees and leaves and bark.
Sometimes he'd lick our pots.

Our dog and he would play outside.
They chased each other around.
The neighbors used to call us up,
"They're shaking up our ground!"

Sometimes we'd let the rhino come
Inside our little house.
If he'd been extra good that week
We'd let him on the couch.

A rhino makes a lovely pet.
They're smart and they obey.
But if you make one REAL mad,
You'll want to run away.

✦ SPECIAL WORDS ✦

bark   each   couch   pet   smart   real

Our Rhino

READING COMPREHENSION

Fill in the blanks with the word that best completes the sentence.

1 Our _____ lived in our backyard.

    hippo   elephant   cat   rhino

2 He ate the trees and leaves and _____ .

    grass   ice cream   bark   dirt

3 Our dog and he would _____ outside.

    sit   play   eat   howl

4 The neighbors would call us up, saying, "They're shaking up our
_____ !"

    house   street   ground   kitchen

5 If he'd been extra good that week, we'd let the rhino on the
_____ .

    couch   chair   bed   rug

RHYME TIME

Circle the words in each column that rhyme with the word in bold. What
other words rhyme with that word? Write them in the spaces below.

bark	**each**	**couch**	**pet**	**smart**	**real**
shark	teach	ouch	met	start	meal
dark	eat	pouch	peel	cart	fell
barn	reach	grouch	let	part	seal

_____ _____ _____ _____ _____ _____

_____ _____ _____ _____ _____ _____

Our Rhino

READL, THINK, DRAW

READ, THINK, DRAW

◆ Draw the rhino.

◆ Give him a bowl of leaves to eat.

WORD WORK

Unscramble the letters to write the words listed in the box below.

| bark | each | couch | pet | smart | real |

krba _____   hcuoc _____

tep _____   ratms _____

hcae _____   aelr _____

Fill in the blanks using the words listed in the box above.

1. If the rhino had been extra good that week, we'd let him on the

_____ .

2. A rhino makes a lovely _____ .

Cleaning the Alligator's Teeth

Use the questions and prompt below to encourage your students to discuss and think about the poem.

Before Reading Questions

1. Why do we go to the dentist?

2. What would the dentist think if you took your pet alligator to the office?

3. If you decided to clean an alligator's teeth in your backyard, what kind of brush would you use?

After Reading Questions

1. Why did the alligator laugh?

2. Would you pinch an alligator? Why or why not?

3. What should the alligator do to keep his teeth healthy?

Writing Prompt

✎ What is the best way to brush an alligator's teeth?

Cleaning the Alligator's Teeth

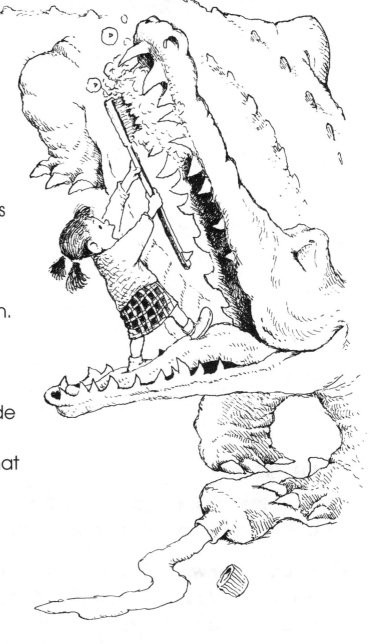

The alligator asked if I
Would clean his dirty teeth.
I climbed inside his jagged jaws
And brushed up underneath.

I felt his two jaws start to close.
His sharp teeth touched my skin.
I yelled, "I'm not a sandwich!
Open up and give a grin!"

The alligator laughed and made
His two jaws open wide.
I said, "The next time you do that
I'll have to pinch your hide."

He gave another 'gator laugh
That shook me head to toe.
I finished brushing all his teeth
And said, "I've got to go."

SPECIAL WORDS

clean	jaws	start	grin	wide	stood

Cleaning the Alligator's Teeth

READING COMPREHENSION

Fill in the blanks with the word that best completes the sentence.

1. The alligator asked if I would brush his dirty _____ .

   claws   teeth   scales   tail

2. I climbed inside his jagged _____ .

   nose   ears   mouth   jaws

3. I felt his two jaws start to _____ .

   open   chew   lick   close

4. His _____ teeth touched my skin.

   many   white   sharp   mean

5. I yelled, "I'm not a sandwich, open up and give a

   _____ ."

   laugh   grin   yell   bite

RHYME TIME

Circle the words in each column that rhyme with the word in bold. What other words rhyme with that word? Write them in the spaces below.

clean	jaws	start	grin	wide	stood
bean	claws	dart	win	slide	good
mean	jam	star	fin	hide	stop
seen	laws	cart	pin	ride	hood
_____	_____	_____	_____	_____	_____
_____	_____	_____	_____	_____	_____

Cleaning the Alligator's Teeth

READD, THINK, DRAW

◆ Draw the alligator's teeth.

◆ Make each tooth very sharp.

WORD WORK

Unscramble the letters to write the words listed in the box below.

| clean | jaws | start | grin | wide | stood |

ediw _____

cneal _____

swaj _____

dsoot _____

trats _____

nirg _____

Fill in the blanks using the words listed in the box above.

☆1 The alligator asked me to _____ his dirty teeth.

☆2 The alligator laughed and made his two jaws open _____ .

The Wolf and the Rabbit

Use the questions and prompt below to encourage your students to discuss and think about the poem.

Before Reading Questions

1. Why is it hard to catch a rabbit?

2. How is a wild rabbit different from a tame rabbit?

3. Which would you rather have as a pet, a wolf or a rabbit?

4. Would a rabbit be easier to raise than a wolf? Why or why not?

After Reading Questions

1. Why do you think that the wolf and the rabbit will never become friends?

2. Why are rabbits and wolves "natural enemies"?

Writing Prompt

✎ If you were a rabbit, how would you try to fool the wolf?

The Wolf and the Rabbit

The wolf howled deep into the night.
The rabbit thought, "Oh no!
That hungry wolf will do her best
To eat me ears to toe."

Just then a wolf jumped from the brush
And snapped at rabbit's head.
The rabbit hopped with all her might
And got away instead.

When rabbit got into her den
She said, "Kids, listen up.
There are hungry wolves outside
Who need to feed their hungry pups."

"So when you hear a howl
Just stop and lie down in the grass
And get your legs and mind in gear
To hop away and fast."

SPECIAL WORDS

night	best	brush	snapped	den	pups

The Wolf and the Rabbit

READING COMPREHENSION

Fill in the blanks with the word that best completes the sentence.

1. The _____ howled deep into the night.

   cat   cow   wolf   owl

2. "That hungry wolf will do her best to eat me ears to _____ ."

   feet   toe   chin   fingers

3. The wolf jumped from the _____ and snapped at rabbit's head.

   tree   rock   brush   hole

4. The rabbit went back to his _____ .

   hill   mother   den   field

5. "There are hungry wolves outside who need to feed their hungry
   _____ ."

   pups   kittens   brothers   sisters

RHYME TIME

Circle the words in each column that rhyme with the word in bold. What other words rhyme with that word? Write them in the spaces below.

night	**best**	**brush**	**snapped**	**den**	**pups**
light	rest	mush	napped	men	cups
bite	bean	crush	snowed	ten	put
fight	test	hush	wrapped	hen	cut
_____	_____	_____	_____	_____	_____
_____	_____	_____	_____	_____	_____

The Wolf and the Rabbit

READ, THINK, DRAW

◆ Draw the wolf howling.

◆ Put a moon in the sky.

WORD WORK

Unscramble the letters to write the words listed in the box below.

night	best	brush	snapped	den	pups

ned   _____

deppasn _____

btse   _____

thgin   _____

supp   _____

hsurb   _____

Fill in the blanks using the words listed in the box above.

1. The wolf howled deep into the _____ .

2. "That hungry wolf will do her _____ to eat me ears to toe,"

Honey Bear

Use the questions and prompt below to encourage your students to discuss and think about the poem.

Before Reading Questions

1. If you wanted to find a cave today, where would you go?

2. Why would a bear want to have a cave for a home?

3. Since there is no bear cave in your backyard, where could you go to see a wild bear?

After Reading Questions

1. Why did the bee sting the bear?

2. Why was it so easy for the bear to climb the tree?

3. How do you think the bear will behave the next time he sees a beehive?

Writing Prompt

✎ Describe three ways the bear and the bees could make peace.

Honey Bear

I walked into the forest.
The sun was high and bright.
But suddenly I tripped and fell
And there was no more light.

I felt my hands and fingers.
All seemed to be okay.
But looking around I realized
I'd fallen in a cave.

I heard some water dripping.
I heard some bats take off.
I heard a big, deep, scary growl
And then a loud bear cough.

I saw off in a corner
A bear upon a bed.
He had a swollen mouth.
I saw a bandage on his head.

I walked up very gently
And asked if he was sick.
He coughed and growled and
Looked at me and said,
"My tongue can't lick."

He said, "It happened last week.
I found a hive of bees.
With golden honey dripping down
I had to climb that tree."

"I threw my head into the hive
And licked with all I had,
And everything was going well
Until it turned quite bad."

"A bee was very angry.
He buzzed, 'We've had enough!'
And then he stung me on my tongue.
His sting hurt me so much!"

"I quickly lost my footing
And fell down to the ground
And that's where my mom said,
Two hours later I was found."

I said, "Bear, I'm so sorry
Your tongue can't even lick.
I hope you get well soon.
I know it's no fun to be sick."

SPECIAL WORDS

| sun | fell | bats | sweet | sick | sting |

Honey Bear

READING COMPREHENSION

Fill in the blanks with the word that best completes the sentence.

1. I walked into the _____ .

   outside   desert   forest   mountain

2. I fell into a _____ .

   crack   cave   well   puddle

3. The bear had a swollen _____ .

   paw   head   mouth   claw

4. I walked up gently and asked if he was _____ .

   tired   sick   weak   happy

5. An angry bee had _____ the bear's tongue.

   bit   stung   hit   chewed

RHYME TIME

Circle the words in each column that rhyme with the word in bold. What other words rhyme with that word? Write them in the spaces below.

sun	**fell**	**bats**	**sweet**	**sick**	**sting**
fun	tell	cats	sheet	stick	wing
done	shell	bags	feet	stop	ring
run	felt	rats	neat	lick	steam
none	sell	hats	heel	pick	thing
_____	_____	_____	_____	_____	_____
_____	_____	_____	_____	_____	_____

Honey Bear

READ, THINK, DRAW

◆ Draw the bear in a cave.

◆ Add three bats to your picture.

WORD WORK

Unscramble the letters to write the words listed in the box below.

| sun | fell | bats | sweet | sick | sting |

tasb _____   teesw _____

nus _____   gnits _____

llef _____   ikcs _____

Fill in the blanks using the words listed in the box above.

1. "I walked into the forest when the _____ was high and bright."

2. "I tripped and _____ and there was no more light."

Notes